FRUIT BASKET

Payam Ghassemlou, Ph.D.

CONTENTS

FRUIT BASKET

When I first met Javid (pseudonym) at the San Francisco LGBT Parade Festival over two decades ago, he was just a happy-go-lucky guy who lived a carefree life. Despite the fact that we did not have much in common at the time, somehow we managed to keep in contact over the years. In his early e-mails, he mostly talked about himself. I found some of his stories amusing. Once in a while, I would give him my two cents about some of his life choices. I have summarized our e-mail exchanges here in order to tell the story of how his life progressed. I am hoping that by sharing these e-mail dialogues, I can inspire others to add more depth and meaning to their lives. Javid's Iranian background adds another beneficial layer. As a gay Iranian living in Los Angeles, I would like to do my part in bringing attention to the challenges gay Iranians (by gay, I refer primarily to the entire LGBT community) experience living in Iran and elsewhere overseas. Also, in my writing, I aim to bring awareness to the issues related to internalized homophobia, and encourage the reader not to minimize the negative impacts of homophobia on the formative experiences of gay people.

"What is the purpose of my life? Why am I here? Where is my life going?" Javid told me that he had been asking himself these questions ever since he stopped denying his need for a meaningful existence. His acknowledgement of that need was an invitation to not only reflect on his life and question its meaning, but also to express his care for other people and the planet. For someone whose entire worth was wrapped up in trying to be young and fabulous, growing older and more purposeless was beginning to feel like a dark night of the soul.

When Javid was in his pleasure-seeking years, his life was one big Disneyland ride of sexual ecstasy and apple martinis. Early on, he was a wild and crazy fool who lived in various gay ghettos. He did crazy things, like barhopping in West Hollywood while dressed as a nun with a dildo hanging from his neck. And then there were those warm summer afternoons with his cute friend Jason in Laguna Beach, when they would climb all the way down a sharp cliff to a secret spot on the beach. They would then swim out to one of the yachts moored a mile from the isolated beach, choose one that was flying a rainbow flag, and seduce the rich owner into taking them for a ride.

Almost every year, Javid danced at the circuit parties in South Beach, surrounded by hot guys wearing nothing but underwear and combat boots. For many summers, he attended pool parties in the Hollywood Hills where he would indulge his senses while the Madonna song "Vogue" rocked from the rafters. Drugs were prevalent at those parties, but Javid never took them. He used to say, "I have my standards."

Javid can still get aroused when sharing about the night on a gay cruise when he met a blond Navy boy from Idaho who introduced himself as Eugene. The boy had never tasted a Middle Eastern dish before, and Javid became his favorite kabob that night. With Javid's brown skin pressed against his pale body, Eugene whispered, "Tonight, I am sleeping with the enemy." Javid whispered back, "Make love to me, not war."

Javid could get bored easily, so he was always on the lookout for new adventures. He tried the Folsom Street Fair in San Francisco. After a few attempts at using a collar and leash, he realized that he was hopelessly vanilla and couldn't fool any hot leather daddies into letting him ride them. He also rarely missed going to the Russian River during Labor Day weekend. There, he could let it all hang out, skinny-dipping in the river late at night. He spent so much time in the river during the night and sunbathing all day that he jokingly referred to himself as a "semi-aquatic homo creature."

Javid had no real career direction or significant relationships. He knew all the salespeople at the Dolce & Gabbana store in town, where he would max out his credit cards. Javid was notorious for talking nonstop about himself, and his attention span was just long enough to follow a short Bloomingdale's commercial. Around the time of his birthday, Javid would drop hints to let his friends know how much

Persian caviar from Petrossian would make him feel connected to the Caspian Sea. He would go on and on, bragging about a time when he was a kid and muscular fishermen would let him fish with them since he looked so adorable.

Javid was drifting on the planet homo with vanity as his travel companion. There is no law against shallowness, but Javid intuitively knew he has unrealized potential. Despite his constant socializing, he began to realize that something in his life was missing. "This shit is getting old," he stated in one of his emails to me. He was sensing a feeling of emptiness that he could no longer cover up with sex, clubbing, and designer clothes. A need for something deeper was emerging inside him. Javid did not need to endure a life-shattering event like a terminal illness to spark this realization. Rather, somewhere in his brain, a few synapses were making the right connections. A light bulb was starting to flicker on. Not everyone needs a dramatic experience to begin a process of self-reflection. For some, the soul simply wakes up, and the heart invites the mind to dance to a more meaningful tune.

LAST DANCE

Javid had his last dance with vanity on the night he attended an after-hours club in San Francisco. The evening began as just another adventure at a cruise-y hole-in-the wall in the middle of the Castro.

Then he noticed his reflection in the big mirror behind Ernesto, the handsome Latin bartender who had failed to call him few months beforehand following a lively flirtation – just another one of Javid's all-too-familiar rejection stories. But tonight, Javid made eye contact only with himself, and saw his soul longing for something meaningful. It didn't make sense to be in a club after 2:00 A.M., looking for some kind of validation in Ernesto's attention. Javid wasn't 22 anymore. Suddenly, he felt the need to leave the gay fraternity. He could no longer lose himself in the small pond he called his "gay adolescence." Now, he asked himself, "Did you come out of the closet just to be seen at the most fabulous parties parading in your white Calvin Klein underwear? Was all that activism, waving your rainbow flag at gay parade marches, just a play for Ernesto's dick?" On the other hand, he replied to himself, "If I stop, I have nothing." For Javid, that conflict represented the beginning of a need for meaning in his life. Life out of the closet was more complicated than he thought, and nothingness was the place to start. It was better to have nothing than to have a shallow life of sensory indulgence. At least with nothing, he had room to add something new.

PEOPLE INSIDE JAVID

Living a small apartment building on a street called Drama, Javid had different people living inside him. He often heard the voice of the Fool in him, joking, "Life must-haves include Martini, credit cards, and access to a Mall." Another one of Javid's inner characters, the Trickster, found delight in being mischievous. He liked to break rules and act scandalously. Prior to our e-mail exchanges, Javid was not aware of this aspect of his personality. Each time the Fool or the Trickster took over, he found himself in trouble. Inspired by Jungian Psychology, I pointed out to him how much our life can be impacted by different archetypes at play in our personality, and encouraged him to become conscious of them.

Javid also has an inner Bitch with a sharp tongue. One time, Javid was standing in a checkout line at grocery store somewhere in the East Village. He was flirting with a man he'd met 20 minutes earlier in the meat department and was trying to get his phone number. An overweight middle-aged woman standing in front of them who was paying for a tall broom overheard their flirting and gave them a dirty look. Javid unleashed his inner Bitch and said to her, "What are you looking at bitch? You better get on that broom and fly the fuck out of here before I shove it up your ass." The look of shock on the other man's face and the look of humiliation in the woman's eyes became Javid's point of contact with his own darker side. Sometimes other people's reactions can point to something dangerous inside us. In his later e-mails, Javid told me that it had taken him many years of psychological labor to tame the inner Bitch and develop a healthier expression of feminine side. Javid has met many gay men with a similarly acid wit, and describes this phenomenon as an epidemic. To this day, the Trickster keeps telling Javid that the homophobic woman deserved humiliation, but his inner Sage reminds him, "Just because you can call someone a bitch doesn't mean you should." Among the many characters within Javid, the Trickster and the Fool were actively in conflict with the Sage. The Sage is the wise part of Javid who wants him to grow up. When the Sage takes charge, Javid becomes a deeper person, asking questions like, "What is the purpose of my life?" or "How can I be more childlike and less childish?" I have always encouraged Javid to embrace his inner Sage, while rehabilitating his other internal characters. The Trickster often jokes, "No rehab center is big enough to accommodate all of Javid's neuroses." However, his Sage jokingly counters, "Don't you worry; I am sure the state hospital has enough beds to admit them all."

GAY ADOLESCENCE

I don't want to sound critical of Javid for undergoing his "gay adolescence" in his twenties and thirties. Many gay people experience adolescence later in life due to homophobia, which prevents many gay youths from discovering and expressing their authentic gay selves. Javid shared with me that when he was an adolescent, he constantly felt a combination of shame and longing in regard to his need for closeness to other boys. The fear of being terrorized by peers prevented him from being himself and becoming a normal, fun-loving teenager. Heterosexual teenage boys could enjoy the freedom of dancing with their girlfriends at school dances; Javid wanted to feel free and joyous like them, but the world that he grew up in did not welcome such behavior. He has never forgotten the day when he found a Jehovah's Witness pamphlet on sexuality at the bus stop near his school. At first he was excited about finding something to read regarding homosexuality, since he was feeling confused and in desperate need of a way to understand himself. However, the messages of hate in that pamphlet made him feel ashamed about his same-sex attraction, and caused him to believe that damnation was the price of his natural feelings.

I felt angry as I listened to Javid relate his struggles with homophobia. It is deeply painful to know what religious bigots can do in the name of God, driving gay youths to self-hatred and suicide by spreading their messages of hate and intolerance in any place of worship they can find. Later on, Javid shared how much repressed anger he has about the humiliation he was made to feel for something as natural as being gay. Unconsciously, he tried to make up for this sense of loss by channeling his rage into a compensatory "fabulous" lifestyle. Wisely, the Sage reminds him, "It was better to live your gay adolescence later in life than to repress that desire." However, Javid was having a difficult time growing beyond that. He was missing his chance to work through the emotions, including grief, that comes with being robbed of what could have been a self-affirming upbringing.

CURIOSITY

As Javid became interested in changing his direction, he saw that he needed a guide to help him live a more authentic and meaningful life. He was not interested in traveling to India or Bali to find a guru. "Instead, let curiosity be your guide," the Sage encouraged him. "Curiosity killed the cat," argued the Trickster. "Shallowness is killing your sense of curiosity. Ignore that voice," the Sage insisted. "Curiosity put in motion a wondrous dance with creation." I stated in one of my emails to him. I wrote to him about curiosity as a powerful emotion that, once activated, can lead to an interesting life. His inner Sage, along with my supportive emails, began to ignite his sense of curiosity.

By opening up to this sense of curiosity, Javid allowed himself to be inquisitive and, for the first time, take an interest in his inner life and the world around him. Previously, his curiosity had been limited to exploring which kind of conditioner would add the most volume to his hair. Now, Javid needed to expand the landscape of his curiosity beyond places like the local mall. Instead, he followed his inner Sage's advice and let his curiosity expose him to soulful places like museums, nature, poetry readings, introspective moments, creative writing classes, anti-war rallies, meditation groups, and AIDS and pro-environmental organizations in need of volunteers. Curiosity as an emotion added richness to his life, pulling him out of his limited party boy life style.

Slowly, his curiosity began to develop a life of its own. A power beyond his old self kept pushing him to wake up to a more inquisitive lifestyle. Javid was being drawn toward different life experiences needed for his growth. Curiosity was more than just an emotion in his case; it was a gift. His heart was longing for something deeper, and he was curious to find that depth.

We also discussed the fact that so few people tap into their sense of curiosity due to the constant distractions of social media, the daily struggle to pay pills, and the endless barrage of shallow television programs. No wonder so many people feel discontent and have trouble living a purposeful life. I wrote to him, "It amazes me how much our local news focuses on car chases, celebrity gossip, and Lotto hysteria." The good news is that subscription to one's "curiosity channel" is free and starts with paying attention to one's life as it unfolds in the moment. Javid was starting to get a lot from his curiosity; it was the driving force he needed to move forward in life.

GAY POLITICS

The only thing Javid used to like about politics was the word *party*. But after attending to his curiosity, Javid began to develop his interest in gay politics, and soon found himself wanting to fight against the discrimination of LGBT people. However, in this pursuit he was dismayed to discover a kind of activism that was mainly focused on assimilation. At the time, many gay activists were saying, "We are like everyone else." This sentiment did not work for Javid, who told me he wanted to be liberated, not assimilated. He knew that, as a gay person, he was different, and he wanted to let that difference help him transcend social norms and reach another level of consciousness. "I feel I can have more empathy for other people who are suffering from any type of discrimination because of my own experiences with discrimination," he declared. Javid started to support his community's struggle for equal rights by donating money to marriage equality causes, writing letters to officials, and attending pro-gay marches. Reading about Javid's progress in personal growth, I was impressed. His e-mails to me were starting to reveal a totally different person. Javid's Trickster jokingly exaggerated his process of change as "The extreme makeover of Queen Marie Antoinette." In response, Javid's inner Sage shouted back, "Eat cake, Trickster."

GAY PSYCHOLOGY

As time went on, Javid's relationship to his gayness became less and less political. Working on himself through personal analysis was helping him to gain more psychological insight about his orientation; in this way, Javid was becoming a deeper person. By developing a psychological perspective on gay liberation, not merely a political one, he was opening a new frontier in his struggle for equal rights. I shared with him that the gay civil rights movement is like a bird that needs two wings to fly, not just one. So far, the political wing has been the main carrier of this movement. By adding psychological healing work as the other wing, the bird of gay liberty can reach even greater heights. Javid agreed with me, writing about how psychological approaches to gay liberation need to involve dealing with internalized homophobia. Gays and lesbians can grow by participation in such a psychological process. These techniques can help them to take pride in their identity. With frustration in his tone, Javid told me that he'd met gay men who told him they had never experienced shame or homophobia growing up. "I don't know which planet they grew up on. It must be the Planet Homo somewhere in the galaxy where I was not invited because they already had a queen," he complained.

Internalized homophobia consists of rejection and shame. Javid was forced to experience both of these growing up in an anti-gay society, and, in particular, as a school-aged child. He found that an effective way to liberate himself from homophobia was to challenge it internally. Javid had to let go of using words such as "straight acting" or the belief that "others are going to think less of me because I am gay."

We exchanged emails on how having a psyche contaminated by internalized homophobia can lead to self-hatred and self-destructive behavior such as drug and alcohol abuse, risky sex, domestic violence, and suicide. It was refreshing to have such meaningful conversations with him, as I used to get bored reading about Javid's never-ending relationship dramas. Sometimes he would write pages upon pages about disappointing dating episodes, yet show no clear insight or sense of self-awareness. I welcomed our deeper exchanges.

Based on the personal work he was doing, Javid began to identify the concept of the inner child as a valuable healing tool that has helped him to personify his repressed childhood feelings and have empathy for them. Javid's gay inner child wanted so desperately to tell his story of growing up in a world where he was put down and teased for being a "sissy." He felt alone and suffered in silence as a school-aged child. He came to believe that working psychologically with his pain could transform those feelings and give birth to new ones. "Loving my inner kid is making me a better person," Javid added. He continued, "There is more to being gay than what my inner Bitch wants me to believe." I encouraged him to develop compassion for all parts of himself— including the inner Bitch—and start a dialogue with her through the use of active imagination. Perhaps this part of Javid has a story to share, and can be transformed through understanding.

DESPERATELY SEEKING BOYFRIEND

One of Javid's earlier e-mails to me was about a particular dating episode. When Javid moved back to Los Angeles for the third time because he could not decide whether to live in LA or San Francisco, he was desperately seeking a boyfriend. He had even designed a t-shirt that read, "Lift the embargo on Iran. DATE ME." That was before he met his current life partner at a yogurt shop in West Hollywood and began the soul searching that I have been writing about here.

In his attempt to increase his chances of finding a boyfriend, Javid went to Book Soup on Sunset Boulevard and bought one of those New Age books on dating. I was shocked when Javid told me he finished reading the book, as he had never before read anything longer than reviews on gay porn. The book advised Javid to make his bedroom more welcoming to create a sense of "Eros." So he redecorated his bedroom and took down his beloved Ricky Martin poster. He got rid of his queen-size bed from IKEA and purchased a California king-size from one of the fancy furniture stores on Melrose Avenue, hoping that a new, bigger bed would put a welcoming energy out in to the universe, giving him a better chance of finding a boyfriend.

The new bed, black satin sheets, red candles, dim lighting, romantic landscape painting on the wall, custom-made window treatments, designer condom box, and state-of-the-art sound system (ready to turn up "Come, come, come into my world") made the bedroom "fabulous." He was prepared to commence his mission: capture a future husband and release him into this impeccably-decorated bedroom. "He will fall in love with me and we live happily ever after," Javid was certain.

Javid met Amir soon afterwards – not in a singles bar but at the National Gay Soccer Tournament in Los Angeles. A few years earlier, Javid had joined a gay soccer team in San Francisco because he was attracted to guys in soccer outfits. Amir was a sexy young Arab doctor, who looked especially sexy in soccer shorts. Javid inquired about my thoughts on a Persian dating an Arab. "Javid," I told him, "As gay people, we are connected through our hearts. We are all in the same boat, regardless of our race or country of origin. Let's celebrate our gay connection, which runs deeper than political conflicts." Then his Trickster jumped in, saying, "As long as he is hung and good in bed, we don't care about race." "Considering how many things are wrong with Trickster, it's at least nice to know he's not racist," the Sage added to the conversation.

Amir accepted Javid's invitation to go on a date. The second week into their dating, Javid found the right opportunity to ask Amir to spend the weekend at his place. Javid figured his new bed would bring him luck. Prior to Amir's arrival, Javid bought cupcakes from CAKE

AND ART, delicious organic food from Whole Foods Market, and Persian ice cream from Mashti Malone's.

In an e-mail to Javid, I asked him why he was doing all that preparation for Amir. In his reply, he described his gay enactment of the Oedipal complex, stating, "I had this flashback of my mother preparing my father's favorite dish to earn his love. This is the only way I know how to be with a guy." Javid also confided in me his yearning to be loved by his father, while unconsciously over-identifying with his mother's way of getting his father's attention, which did not work.

On the weekend that Amir was at his house, Javid's new bed became the crossroads of a lot of different feelings, many rooted in the past. "I think you are a great guy, but I just don't feel the chemistry between us," Amir declared as he lay in Javid's new bed. "Whatever," Javid responded coldly in order to cover up his hurt feelings. The weekend ended with Amir saying politely, "Thank you for your hospitality, Javid."

The frustration of not being validated by Amir gave rise to feelings that had been buried in Javid for a long time. At first, he blamed himself for being too needy and desperate. Then he blamed Amir for having a fear of intimacy and playing games. Eventually, he began to discuss those feelings in our later e-mail exchanges.

Javid and I discussed how being rejected by Amir felt humiliating and provoked a hurt place within him that had been repressed since he was a child. He recalled a distant time when he was in elementary school and felt painfully alone. His peers called him sissy and wouldn't play with him. At home, his father kept his distance since Javid was not a typical masculine boy; instead, Javid enjoyed playing with his mother's wigs. Javid needed to heal this emotional wound in order to be able to tolerate the roller coaster of dating that most adults must endure in order to find the right partner. "Dating has always been a hellish experience for me," he recalled.

Javid also added that he knew the need to have Amir as a boyfriend came from a lonely and desperate place; he didn't think it was all about "Eros." Rather, his desire was more about the embarrassment he felt as a result of being single. Javid hated when his friends would ask him, "How come you are still single?" or tell him, "Don't worry, you'll find a boyfriend." Javid refused to accept their pity. He was so caught up in his negative feelings surrounding his loneliness that he could not enjoy anything unless he could share it with a "boyfriend." It was as if Javid did not exist unless he was in a relationship.

I quoted Javid the following poem by Rumi (translated by Coleman Barks):

"The minute I heard my first love story, I started looking for you.

Not knowing how blind that was. Lovers don't finally meet
somewhere.

They are in each other all along."

Inspired by Rumi's words, I shared with him that there is another kind of love affair that takes place inside one's heart. A breakup or a romantic relationship can serve as preparation for such mystical love affair. At the time, even though Javid did not completely understand what I was writing to him, I could see that Rumi's words still had a powerful impact.

COMING OUT OF TOXIC SHAME

We all have an internal dialogue consisting of elements that are relevant to our lives. Oftentimes, the inner conversation about being gay can be influenced by one's past negative experiences with homophobia. Many of those memories are stored in the psyche in the form of implicit memory: a type of memory that impacts one's life without one noticing it or consciously knowing its origin. Healing from toxic shame involves making implicit memory more conscious, becoming aware of the repressed or disassociated memories and feelings around homophobic mistreatment. I encouraged Javid to give voice to the experiences of his gay inner child by sharing with people that made him feel safe.

All the rejection and derogatory name-calling Javid suffered as a child is stored in his memory bank. His feelings and perspective about himself as a gay person are influenced by those negative memories. With the help and support of his therapist, Javid began a process of coming out of toxic shame. For Javid, this process involved recalling and sharing what it felt like growing up gay in a world that did not respect his gayness, feeling fully the injustice of it. Providing empathy and unconditional positive regard for the fact that he had endured many years of confusion, shame, fear, and homophobic mistreatment gave birth to new feelings of pride and honor toward his gayness. Javid's therapist helped him to understand this as an "alchemical process that involves transforming painful emotions through love and empathy." This psychological purification strengthened Javid's relationship with his gay self, helping him dive deeper into the ocean of his unconscious and redeem his divine essence.

"You mean his Diva essence," Javid's Trickster wrote back.

"Sounds like this Sage guy has been watching too much Oprah," joined the Fool.

"Enough, you two," ordered the Sage.

IRAN

I once asked Javid what it was like to witness revolution and war as a teenager living in Iran. At first he gave a shallow response: "Watching men in army uniform was a turn on." I appealed to his wiser self for something more meaningful, to which he replied, "Every time I asked to look back, my mind gets flooded with images of people running for safety." He continued, "I can remember taking shelter in the basement with family and neighbors. The sound of explosions coming from two blocks away filled me with terror. I reached inside my pocket for a Valium that I found the day before hidden in my mother's nightstand. It must have been the maximum dosage, because my heart stopped racing a short while after taking it."

The experiences of war that he shared left me with sadness and a strange sense of guilt. It then dawned on me that this guilty feeling did not belong to me, but rather belonged to those who wage wars and make profit by selling weapons at the expense of innocent lives. "Shame on them," I thought, and with that, I let go of my guilt.

On the topic of revolution, Javid stated, "There is something very innocent about people participating in a revolution hoping for democracy. It saddens me that in the name of God people can get manipulated into endorsing religious leadership that leads them into the dark ages." I agreed, stating, "Many religious and political figures exploit people's innocence by using highly charged words like Jihad or crusade and throw them into emotional frenzy. In this way, they steer people away from reaching true freedom."

Javid began to open up more about his frustration with religious bigotry, stating, "There should be separation between the mosque and state. Organized religion is the opiate of the masses, and rarely anything good comes out of it. A mullah who hates gays is no different than a homophobic priest who preaches anti-gay messages. When it comes to oppression of gays and lesbians, all fundamentalists, regardless of their religious affiliation, go to bed with each other." I did not delve too much into religious discussions with him because we had more important topics to embrace. Everyone needs to find his or her own path to enlightenment, and organized religion was not Javid's path.

We also considered possible solutions to current world crises, such as climate change or income inequality. Javid stated, "The problem with the world has to do with lack of LGBT leaders. If more of us were in leadership positions, the world would be in better shape." I shared with Javid how wonderful it would be to have a gay president in the White House. Javid agreed, stating, "I am sure that would be a nicely decorated White House with great lighting, and a discotheque inside for all the world leaders to dance together instead of waging war against each other." Javid thought of gays (and lesbians as well) as the pinnacle of evolution.

RACE

As a foreign-born gay man living in the U.S., Javid wanted to feel included, but at the same time, he was forced to deal with prejudice. Despite his militant inner Bitch who at times confronted discrimination, deep down he felt that others looked down on him because of his nationality. Since Western media focuses mostly on negative news from the Middle East, most Americans get the wrong impression about the region. This bothered Javid, and he felt powerless to change public opinion. He sensed that, for the most part, any person of color who is regularly exposed to U.S. media can start to feel invisible. Javid and I exchanged many emails about a lack of diversity in the media. We discussed how the U.S. media rarely shows people of color as heroes. Movies often portray people of color, especially Middle Easterners, as villains. During the Cold War, the villains were often Communists. Today, for many Westerners, the Middle East is the new scapegoat for their shadow (or dark side, as it is known Jungian psychology). Americans can never own their shadow if they keep projecting it onto the Middle East. Javid wrote, "Originally, Muslim fundamentalists were strengthened by the West to prevent Communism from spreading in to the Middle East. The West should take responsibility for their part in creating this mess."

PERSIAN HERITAGE

Javid was smart enough to know that he could not solve the problem of racial discrimination in America. All he could do was clean his own side of the street by learning more about his own heritage and abstaining from judging others. And so, Javid let his curiosity take him closer to his Persian roots and his gay ancestors. Learning about the richness of Persian literature helped him to take pride in his heritage. He strengthened his grasp of Farsi so that he could go directly to the source instead of reading heterosexist translations of Persian poems. Javid told me, "When I need validation for gay love, I read love poems by Sadi, Hafiz, Rumi, and other Persian poets." I agreed with Javid, and wrote to him that these poets have written many love poems on same-sex desire, indicating that a great deal of Persian literature is based on homosexuality. It saddens me to know that many English translations of classical Persian literature are misleading and do not speak the truth. For example, many poems by Hafiz are translated to make it seem like he is addressing a woman. In reality, Hafiz always honored same-sex love in his poetry. Rumi also wrote many poems to express his love for Shams. Similarly, many translations and interpretations of Rumi's poems are not accurate. Learning about the homoerotic aspects of Persian literature and reading the poetry and life stories of many Sufi poets helped Javid develop an Eastern spiritual connection to his homosexuality.

I felt honored to witness Javid's transformation and his journey into his soul. It was amazing how much Javid was changing the direction of his life, and his process inspired me to continue working on my own journey of self-discovery.

JUNGIAN PSYCHOLOGY

As Javid continued to embrace his sense of curiosity, he became interested in Jungian psychology. Javid's curiosity led him to books by Carl Jung, including *Memories, Dreams, Reflections*. In this autobiography, Javid discovered many gems, including Jung's process of introspection. Such reading inspired Javid to participate in Jungian studies and workshops, which helped him to translate his emotions into images as a way of working with them. He used drawing, painting, collages, writing, poetry, dance movement, and active imagination as a means of honoring his emotions. This alchemical process of translating his raw emotions into meaningful images and insights for the purpose of individuation became an important part of Javid's growth. I deeply appreciated his use of this quote by Jung at the end of one of his emails to me: "As far as we can discern, the sole purpose of human existence is to kindle a light in the darkness of mere being."

Carl Jung's writing helped Javid to understand the importance of approaching the unconscious through dream work. Javid began to pay attention to his dreams and kept a dream journal. He shared with me how he decided to be creative with the cover of his first dream journal and decorate it with meaningful images. By beautifying his dream journal, he was sending an invitation to the dream maker in his unconscious. At first, Javid found dream work challenging. He could not understand the meaning of his dreams, and his rational mind would become frustrated. "Paying attention to your dreams," I reminded him, "even if you don't always understand them, is helping you to form a bridge between consciousness and the unconscious. Everyone needs to take time to construct this bridge in order to invite visitors from the unconscious." Depth psychology has taught Javid that growth and change accelerate when consciousness emerges from the unconscious.

Javid shared many dreams with me after realizing the importance of dream work. In one of his dreams, he was in his therapist's office, which was dark and unlit. Suddenly, his therapist noticed that the room was dark and turned on all the lights. Everything began to look bright and visible to Javid. In my short response to this dream, I stated, "I am glad your therapeutic process is helping you to see things more clearly." It was nice to see that Javid's participation in psychotherapy was bringing more light to his life, enabling him to become a more conscious person. This dream likely also had something to do with the nature of his therapeutic relationship. Javid shared the dream with his therapist, and it opened many dialogues about their work together. Out of respect for his therapeutic journey, I never inquired about his sessions; I always let him to decide how much he was willing to share about his therapy.

Deep psychological labor helped Javid to rehabilitate his inner characters like the Fool and the Trickster, allowing them to more or less to submit to the will of his authentic Self. Javid jokingly told me, "I am still working on overthrowing the Queen in me. She is hanging on tight to her tiara." Javid stopped castrating his male friends by calling them bitches. With the aid of the Sage, he began to tap into his inner wisdom and build a stronger foundation for his life. Javid's true masculinity began to emerge with the help of his Warrior archetype, which he learned to access in his therapy. He also avoided giving in to his inner Bitch and instead let a healthy expression of his femininity emerge. Over time, he shifted his focus towards progress, rather than perfection. "I can keep working on myself until the cows come home. At some point, I need to accept the good, the bad, and the inflated Queen," Javid explained.

Psychological work became Javid's royal road to a spiritual inner space. By polishing the mirror of his heart through psychological inner work, he readied himself for the realm of the transpersonal. The more he liberated himself from toxic shame, the more space he created for mystical encounters. Javid felt as if he was being guided toward what he needed for his spiritual growth. He read spiritual books that left him intoxicated with certain divine knowledge, finally locating the food that could end his spiritual starvation.

SPIRITUALITY

After a yearlong break from regular correspondence, Javid finally wrote to me on the topic of spirituality. I was eager to learn about Javid's spiritual perspective. I understood this was not an easy topic for Javid to write about, as many LGBT people have had negative experiences with anything having to do with God or religion. The mere mention of God can make many of them feel uncomfortable. Homophobic institutions and politicians have been successful in scaring many gays and lesbians away from a loving connection to God. In a very real way, reclaiming God from organized religions that hold a monopoly on God is a form of activism. LGBT people can have their own direct relationship with God and cut out the middleman. This was the case for Javid. With the help of his curiosity, he explored Eastern spirituality. He began to knock on his inner door through meditation and other spiritual practices. Javid learned from Eastern spiritual traditions, including Sufism, that worship takes place in one's heart. He often referred to God as his Beloved, and he was inspired by Rumi's poetry to view worship as a love affair.

Javid went a step beyond traditional spirituality and incorporated being gay as a path toward God—his Beloved. He stated, "Meditation that focuses on passionate love energy in my heart is an intoxicating way to remember the God of my understanding." He added, "This is how I experience 'pilgrimage around the Kaaba of my heart.'"

I asked him, "What ignites this passion in your heart?"

He replied, "Beauty, which includes my attraction to a hot man." He elaborated, "I can walk into a crowded gay hot spot and see God's beauty in the faces of His creations."

"Does that mean all your trips to gay bars were like a holy pilgrimage?" asked the Fool jokingly.

"Here he goes again," said the Sage, annoyed. "I thought we rehabilitated this guy."

During our email exchanges on spirituality, it was very clear that Javid's connection to God had become magnetized through his relationship to his gay soul. Javid described how making love to a man can take place on two levels. One level is about embracing homoerotic feelings and experiencing romantic love. On a deeper level, one can let the lovemaking experience be a point of contact with the Beloved. The ecstasy of lovemaking can become part of one's spiritual process. Javid wrote, "Sometimes the best time to pray is when you are having sex."

"In that case, let's pray more often," recommended the Trickster.

Javid was also learning that, like a veil, lust can prevent a person from having a mystical experience with God. This often happens when one falls into the darkness of sexual compulsion. Reading Jung and drawing from the concept of projection, Javid knew that many gay men tend to channel their hunger for spiritual elevation into meaningless sexual encounters or substance abuse. The never-ending cycle of chasing one's projection in bath houses or online precludes access to an inner space where sexuality can be honored as a way to worship the God of one's understanding.

Javid also tried other meaningful experiences, such as joy in friendships, artistic expression, and deep meditation in his attempts to be with his Beloved. "Even in dark moments of grief and sorrow, one can be with Him," he wrote.

I was glad to learn that Javid's approach to spirituality had nothing do with getting caught up in dogma. In one of his e-mails to me, he stated, "I understand many people believe in the God of their own understanding. No one should impose his or her beliefs onto others. I escaped a country that demands, 'Either you worship our god or we kill you.' In the United States, there is a growing movement of homophobic fundamentalists, who in my view are as scary as the Taliban. They want to take away our rights, and that is upsetting to me."

Javid and I exchanged many emails about his spiritual progression. At first, it seemed obvious to him that, for a long time, he had associated God with homophobic institutions; therefore, he could not have a loving relationship with God. Once he developed his own understanding of God – his Beloved – it deepened his spiritual journey.

VOLUNTEER WORK

Javid's new spiritual path involved service through volunteer work, and I encouraged him to give some of his time to help Mother Earth. Javid agreed; his inner Queen tossed out her tiara and traded her Chanel dress for overalls and construction boots when Javid joined a volunteer crew to clean up after BP's oil spill. Volunteer work was part of Javid's effort to practice humility and helping others. This was a big step for someone with so long a history of being self-involved. Once he arrived at the Louisiana shoreline, he was shocked and disgusted by how BP was getting away with perpetrating such tremendous environmental damage. The images of birds, sea turtles, and dolphins covered in oil were too painful for him to handle, and witnessing that level of devastation threw him into a deep depression. He began to have doubts about the existence of God or anything good in the world, and considered returning home. I encouraged him to channel his anger and not give in to depression. I told him such crimes against nature were done by BP, not God, and encouraged him to hold the appropriate party responsible. He agreed to channel his feelings into actively helping to save the wildlife there. He also participated in a letter writing campaign to protest against BP. Instead of prematurely terminating his work, he remained longer with the cleanup volunteers, which led to a diminishment of his helpless feelings and an overall growth of empowerment.

I validated Javid's anger that BP was able to avoid real punishment for its crimes. Although many years have passed since the oil spill, the deleterious effects on the environment continue. Javid wrote many frustrated emails about this. In one, he said, "It is sad to know that many people spend countless hours writing reviews about restaurants or places they shop, but they hardly pay any attention to crimes against nature." He admitted, "Being part of the solution feels a lot more empowering than helplessly sitting around and getting depressed about such disasters."

DUSTING OFF THE MIRROR

Javid's process started when he awakened to a yearning for a deeper existence. His psychological inner work helped him to conduct an internal housecleaning. Javid explained to me that all the negative events in his past had covered his heart with the dust of inadequate feelings, repressed rage, and resentment. Psychological work, spiritual practices, and volunteer work have helped him to dust off the mirror of his heart so that it could reflect love and kindness once more. He noted the famous saying in many Sufi-related literatures: "God said, 'I am a Hidden treasure. I wanted to be known, so I created the Universe in order to be known.'" Javid added, "My spiritual teaching is helping me to realize that I am here to remember the Beloved and to let my heart reflect His light."

One day at a time, Javid's lifestyle became about keeping his mind and body healthy, being of service to others, and remembering God in his heart.

LAST STOP

After his spiritual awakening, Javid's earlier questions regarding the purpose or meaning of life no longer needed to be asked. He stated, "This is the last stop, and I don't think I will ever leave this spiritual station. Since its depths are limitless, I will be descending for the rest of my life. I am grateful for the grace of curiosity for taking me to this station. This is all I need for this lifetime. In the previous stations, I was working hard to become something. I am here to become nothing."

Javid's journey within was rewarded by the liberation he began to experience by being "in the world but not of the world." He reported, "I still like going out dancing, traveling, and having nice things." His Fool interrupted by saying, "Thank God, for a minute I thought we were moving to a cave in the Himalayas." The Sage laughed in response to the Fool and stated, "Some things never change." "But I don't define myself by those things," Javid ended.

SAYING GOODBYE

Midway through our exchanges, I thought about compiling the emails in order to write about Javid's transformation. I asked Javid what he would like me to title it, and his inner Fool responded, "Fuck, Love, Pray." His inner Sage did not agree with that title, and recommended that I title it, "Fruit Basket." I was intrigued by this suggestion, so I meditated on it. It seems that each email we sent to each other was like a fruit with its own unique texture, color, and taste. It made sense to call this writing project Fruit Basket. I hope readers enjoy its offerings.

Ultimately, Javid decided to stop the frequent email exchanges about his life journey. He wanted to make life less about himself and more about what he could offer to others. I respected his wish, and thanked him for letting me witness his psycho-spiritual journey. I was deeply touched by Javid's transformation; the love in Javid's heart had served him well as a navigator, helping him to no longer be lost.

As a sign of my gratitude, I wrote him a short poem:

Live like a river:

Flow freely

Don't get attached to anything

Nourish life on your path

And finally merge with the Divine ocean of love.

When I last heard from them, Javid and his husband were living a life filled with happiness, depth, and meaning.

I really appreciate you reading my book!

© Payam Ghassemlou MFT Ph.D. is a licensed Marriage and Family Therapist (Psychotherapist) in private practice in West Hollywood, California.

www.DrPayam.Com

www.ingramcontent.com/pod-product-compliance
Lightning Source LLC
Chambersburg PA
CBHW051050030426
42339CB00006B/284